CW00346774

by the same author

He's Not Naughty!
A Children's Guide to Autism
Deborah Brownson MBE
Illustrated by Ben Mason
ISBN 978 1 78592 872 7
eISBN 978 1 78592 873 4

Life Will Never Be Dull

The Little Book of Autism Adventures

Deborah Brownson MBE

Illustrated by Michelle Rebello-Tindall

First published in Great Britain in 2020 by Jessica Kingsley Publishers
An Hachette Company
1

Front cover image source: Michelle Rebello-Tindall.

A CIP catalogue record for this title is available from the British Library and the Library of Congress

ISBN 978 1 78775 322 8
eISBN 978 1 78775 323 5

Printed and bound in Great Britain by Bell & Bain Ltd

Jessica Kingsley Publishers' policy is to use papers that are natural, renewable and recyclable products and made from wood grown in sustainable forests. The logging and manufacturing processes are expected to conform to the environmental regulations of the country of origin.

Jessica Kingsley Publishers
73 Collier Street
London N1 9BE, UK
and
400 Market Street, Suite 400
Philadelphia, PA 19106, USA

www.jkp.com

Dedicated to Gareth, Josh and Jake

– *Deborah*

Dedicated to Oli, Lauren, James and Emily

– *Michelle*

An autism diagnosis is life changing.

Some people may be devastated...

...and some may refuse to accept it.

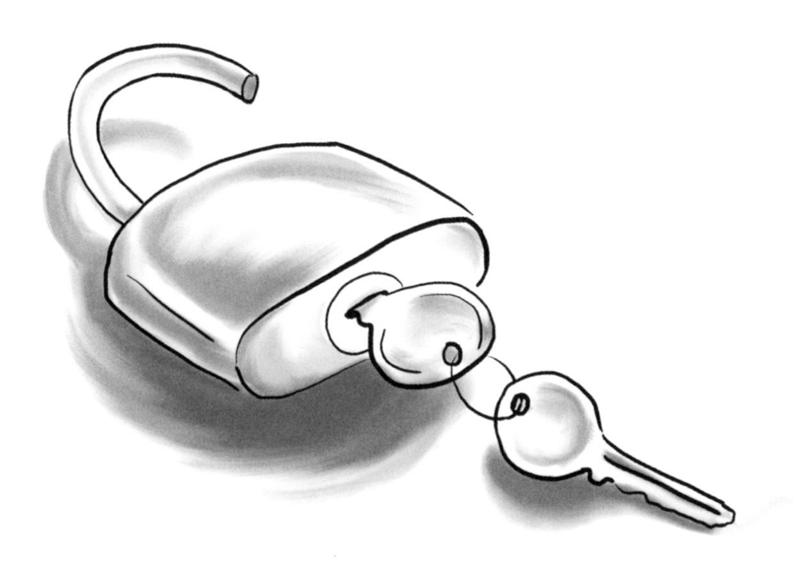

But others are relieved.

It feels like your whole world has
been turned upside down.

You want to cry.

You want to hide.

You want to run away...

...because you don't have the answers.

But autism was always here...

...and your child is the same child.

Your child needs you!

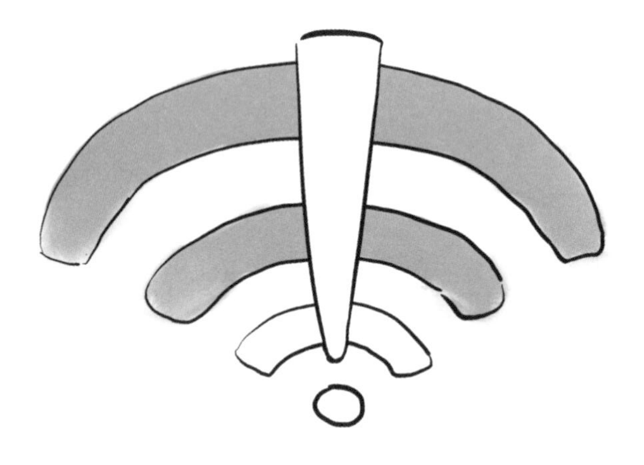

It's not the end of the world...

...but the start of a new adventure.

Tomorrow is a new day.

It's time to find your path...

...and see a different perspective.

Life will never be dull.

You will never be bored...

...and clothing *will be* optional!

As will sleep...

...and earplugs!

Fake friends will disappear...

...as will sanity.

Family may not understand.

True friends become family.

But don't write people off...

...for one day they might surprise you.

You realize what's important in life...

Love

Loyalty

Empathy

Respect

So **cling** to each of them.

Look after yourself.

Remember to be you.

Pursue your dreams.

Accept help.

Learn to say 'No'.

Surround yourself with energy givers.

Learn which battles to fight.

Ignore what people think.

Trust your gut instinct...

...and don't forget to celebrate
each tiny achievement!

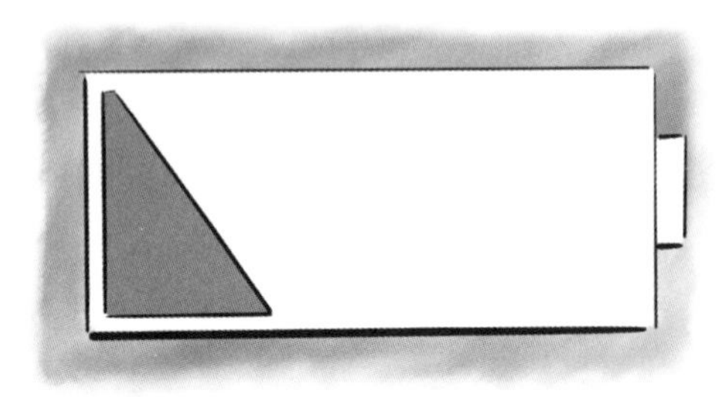

Some days it will all feel too much.

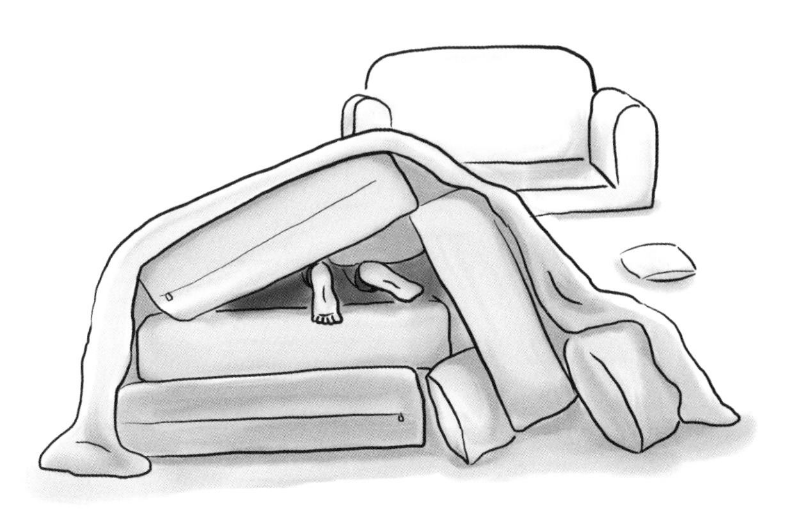

A sense of humour definitely helps...

...as does p a t i e n c e...

...and coffee...

...and wine...

...a housekeeper...

...a nanny...

...four pairs of eyes...

...copious amounts of chocolate...

Oh...and did I mention wine?!

There will be tears...

...and there will be lots of laughs...

...uplifting surprises...

...and air-punching moments of pride!

All of which you can't really appreciate...

...unless you experience the lows.

So, take a deep breath...

...smile.

You are everything your child needs.

You'll get through this.

You'll find your normal.

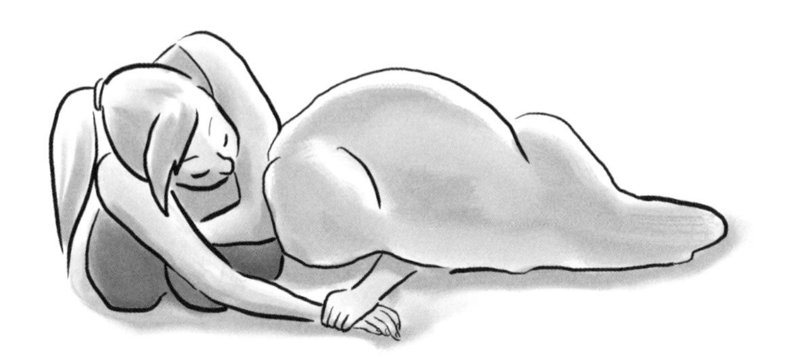

You are your child's best advocate.

Help them lead the way.

Look how far you've come!

Autism adventures await!

ABOUT THE AUTHOR AND ILLUSTRATOR

Deborah Brownson MBE is a writer, solicitor and proud mother of two autistic sons. She received an MBE for her dedication to global autism awareness. She lives in the Lake District, UK.

Michelle Rebello-Tindall is an autistic speaker, illustrator and Autism Ambassador. She is Involvement and Engagement Coordinator and a member of the award-winning autism-friendly team at Dimensions. She founded a group called Autism Adventures – Minecraft and Meltdowns. She has three autistic children and lives in Dorset, UK.